FOCUS ON THE FAMILY ®

HELP!
MY CHILD IS STRUGGLING IN SCHOOL

HELP!
MY CHILD IS STRUGGLING IN SCHOOL

dr. bill maier
general editor

grant l. martin, ph.d.
author

Tyndale House Publishers, Inc.
Carol Stream, Illinois

A Focus on the Family book published by Tyndale House Publishers, Carol Stream, Illinois 60188

TYNDALE and Tyndale's quill logo are registered trademarks of Tyndale House Publishers, Inc.

Edited by: Kathy Davis
Cover design by: Joseph Sapulich
Cover photograph © by Peter Cade/Getty Images. All rights reserved.

Library of Congress Cataloging-in-Publication Data
Martin, Grant.
  Help! my child is struggling in school / Grant Martin.
    p. cm.
  "A Focus on the Family book."
  "This text is excerpted and adapted from Help! my child isn't learning, by Dr. Grant Martin, (c)1995."
  Includes bibliographical references.
  ISBN-13: 978-1-58997-171-4
  ISBN-10: 1-58997-171-X
  1. Learning disabled children—Education—United States. 2. Learning disabilities—United States. 3. Attention-deficit-disordered children—Education—United States. 4. Attention-deficit hyperactivity disorder—United States. 5. Education—Parent participation—United States. I. Martin, Grant. Help! my child isn't learning. II. Title.
  LC4705.M39 2006
  371.9—dc22

                                2006011936

Printed in the United States of America
1 2 3 4 5 6 7 8 9 / 12 11 10 09 08 07 06

Contents

Foreword

Your eight-year-old daughter's teacher has just told you that she may have a learning disability. Your teenage son, who has always been a good student, just brought home a report card full of D's. You've received a letter from the school psychologist at your child's elementary school recommending that your son be tested for ADHD.

If you're a parent who has recently experienced one of these situations or something similar, you may be in a state of shock. What should you do? What does this mean for your child's future? Where can you turn for help?

This book, written by Dr. Grant Martin,

will provide you with solid answers to your many questions. It will guide you through the complicated maze of learning disabilities, attention-deficit disorders, and emotionally related achievement problems. Utilizing clear, easy to understand definitions and diagnostic checklists, the book will help you hone in on what may be responsible for your child's educational struggles.

Dr. Martin will also tell you how to get your child the specialized educational services that he or she may require—services that you may be entitled to under state or federal law. Perhaps most importantly, he'll provide you with the hope and encouragement you need as you face the challenges that may lie ahead.

May the Lord grant you wisdom and discernment as you seek to help your child develop every ounce of his or her God-given potential!

Dr. Bill Maier
Vice President, Psychologist in Residence
Focus on the Family

What Is
a Learning
Problem?

Cheryl's grades have fallen drastically over the past six months. She used to be a happy kid, but now she seems moody and gets into conflicts with the other kids at school. The teacher says she can't figure out what's wrong. Cheryl's father and I have recently started a trial separation; could that be taking a larger toll than we thought?

ↄ ↄ ↄ

Casey just slides along in school, getting mostly Cs, when I know he can do better. He complains that he's bored in school and refuses to keep up with homework assignments. Is there some way I can help him try harder?

ↄ ↄ ↄ

I stopped taking Adam shopping or out in public months ago. I spent all my time policing him, keeping him from running up and down the aisles and wrecking the merchandise. He's getting ready for kindergarten, and I have no idea how they are going to handle him. What should I do?

ᕮ ᕮ ᕮ

Amy daydreams constantly in school. She is almost never in trouble for things like disobedience or talking too much. But she gets consistently low grades because she doesn't complete or turn in her homework. Why can't she focus?

ᕮ ᕮ ᕮ

Parents are concerned about their kids and want them to be as successful as possible. And their questions about their kids' struggles with school and learning are as varied as the concerns themselves. If you are frustrated and upset by your child's learning difficulties, remember this: *There is hope and help for you and your family.*

⌒ ⌒ ⌒

This book will provide a quick overview to help you determine whether your child has a learning problem. Then it will guide you toward more comprehensive help. We'll discuss learning disabilities; attention deficits; emotional barriers such as stress, depression, and family problems; and underachievement. First let's examine common learning difficulties and ways to identify your child's specific problems.

Learning Disabilities

A learning disability is likely a problem of neurological origin that affects specific areas of learning and behavior in an otherwise competent person. A learning disability is *not* a result of emotional disturbance, mental retardation, or hearing, vision, or other sensory impairments such as cerebral palsy. A learning disability can, however, coexist with other handicapping conditions.

The areas of learning that are affected may include the input, output, storage, retention, retrieval, or processing of information. That means a student can have difficulty acquiring, remembering, organizing, recalling, or expressing information.

Learning Styles Compared with Learning Disabilities

Each student has certain methods of learning that work best for him or her.[1] Some students learn best using a visual approach, others are auditory learners. Some are kinesthetic and learn best by doing rather than by seeing or listening. Learning *styles* describe how each person receives and processes information differently. Learning *disabilities* are specific deficits in a student's ability to learn, in contrast to his or her potential. One's learning style can be seen as his or her general pattern of strengths; learning disabilities are specific areas of weakness. To help a student, it's important to understand his or her strengths as well as liabilities.

Attention-Deficit/Hyperactivity Disorder

Some students have trouble learning because they have problems with attention, impulse control, and overarousal. This collection of problematic features is currently called *attention-deficit/hyperactivity disorder* (ADHD).

Clinical experience and research strongly suggest there are three categories of attention disorders—inattentive only, hyperactive/impulsive only, and both inattentive and hyperactive/impulsive (combined type). Most attention-deficit children are *not* hyperactive. Attention-deficit children who are predominantly inattentive tend to be anxious, shy, socially withdrawn, moderately unpopular, poor in sports, and do poorly in school. The inattentive student often stares into space and daydreams, is frequently forgetful in daily activities, appears to be low in energy, and is sluggish and drowsy.

Children who are hyperactive/impulsive can behave in a bizarre and aggressive manner. They often appear to feel no guilt, are unpopular, and perform poorly at school. They seem to have little self-control and are explosive, noisy, disruptive, messy, irresponsible, and immature for their age. These children have a higher-than-normal risk for serious aggressive or rebellious behavior and anti-social acting-out behavior.

Finally, some children can have a combination of both inattention and impulsive-hyperactive features. These kids will have most of the behavioral manifestations of inattention, such as failing to give close attention to details, making careless mistakes, and being easily distracted by extraneous stimuli. In addition, they will often exhibit fidgety hands or feet, inability to remain seated, a tendency to interrupt others, and difficulty awaiting their turn. (For the balance of this book, the abbreviation ADHD will be used for all three types of attention disorders.)

Emotional Barriers to Learning

Emotional difficulties can lower classroom learning, and learning problems can cause a student to react emotionally.

Because of this overlap, distinguishing the learning-disabled student from one who has emotional problems can be tough. Likewise, it's hard to identify the child who has *both* learning problems and emotional difficulties.

The window to a child's inner emotions is his or her behavior. Certain behavioral patterns suggest emotional causes. The *signs* of emotions are easy to see. What they *mean* isn't quite so clear. If we don't know for certain the source of the emotional disturbances, we have to spend time sorting through and diagnosing the issues.

Stress and Its Relationship to Learning Problems

Stress is our body's physical, mental, emotional, and spiritual reaction to circumstances (stressors) that frighten, excite, confuse, endanger, or irritate us. There are three sources of stress for children. The first is everyday frustrations such as homework, relationship tensions, or disagreeable siblings.

The second source is developmental stressors such as entering school or becoming a teenager. These are normal milestones, but they can cause some degree of inner tension as children learn to cope.

The third source of stress is traumatic events over which children have no control, such as parental divorce, sexual abuse, or the death of a loved one. The crisis occurs, and the child must find some way to cope.

Childhood Depression and Learning Problems

Depression can affect people at any age. A child may sleep too much or have insomnia, nightmares, or fitful sleep. Depressed kids may either eat too much or experience a significant loss of appetite. Depression takes away their energy and they no longer want to do those things that previously brought pleasure.

Self-esteem usually deteriorates in depressed children. They don't want to do anything, friends are no longer fulfilling, school is boring, and family is alienated. As a result, they become more despondent and may think about running away or killing themselves.

Depression can be a very natural response to grief, loss, confusion, competition, or stress. It can come from periods of trauma, such as the death of a loved one. Improper diet, inadequate sleep, drugs, infections, and glandular disorders can contribute as well. Whatever the source, depression tells us that something in the person's system needs attention before more serious consequences occur.

Children of Divorce and Learning Problems

Divorce is a double-duty stressor. First, it's a major emotional trauma. It signifies the collapse of the family support and protection system a child needs. As a result, a child's trust in people and permanency is shaken, leaving doubt and uncertainty.

Second, divorce is an accumulative experience. It can last for months or years. Usually, the turmoil doesn't stop after the divorce papers are signed.

Children of divorce must also endure the transition from status quo to single-parent living. They may have to change schools, economic standing, living arrangements, and daily routines. Most children aren't provided with either an adequate explanation or assurance of continued care, which makes the perception of events all the more traumatic.

Family Violence and Learning Problems

Another source of stress, depression, and related emotional problems is abuse and family violence. The pain of abused children can be manifested in many ways, including terrifying nightmares, anxiety, panic attacks, inability to trust, and so on. These manifestations can result whether the children are the direct victims of abuse or just live in homes where violence is inflicted on others.

Abuse may be a real reason why a child isn't learning.[2]

Underachievement

There is perhaps no situation more frustrating for parents than living with children who don't perform up to their academic potential. The problem isn't limited to gifted students; many students don't work up to their potential. Besides underachieving academically, children might also underperform artistically, athletically, or musically.

Many capable children who don't succeed in school are successful in outside activities such as sports, social occasions, and after-school jobs. Even a child who does poorly in most school subjects may display a talent or interest in at least one. Thus, labeling a child as an underachiever disregards any positive outcomes or behaviors the child displays. It's better to label the behaviors rather than the child; for example, the child is "underachieving in math and language arts" rather than an "underachieving student."

Some students (and teachers and

parents) view a passing grade as adequate; there's no underachievement. For others, a B+ could constitute underachievement if the student expected to get an A. Recognizing what constitutes success and failure is the first step toward understanding underachieving behaviors.

Identifying Your Child's Learning Problems

It's time to consider whether your child has the symptoms of a learning problem. The following checklists and descriptions, along with additional information from the teacher and others who are familiar with your child's learning process, will help you begin to identify possible learning difficulties.

Reserve judgment until the evidence seems reasonably clear and a final professional evaluation is made. Your impressions are important, but you also need competent professional input to delineate the exact nature of your child's problems and the probable causes. If the data aren't clear, the symptoms aren't extreme, or the teacher isn't overly concerned, you may want to wait a while to get a better grasp of the situation. Just because a few symptoms from the checklists apply to your child doesn't necessarily mean your child

has a particular problem. Quite a few
symptoms need to be present, along with
definite difficulties in some aspect of
learning.

Questions to Ask If Your Student Isn't Learning

Home-Related Questions

- Can the student's homework routine be made more efficient and productive?
- Could lifestyle factors be affecting the student's school performance? Is the child getting enough sleep, eating well, living in safe conditions, and not watching too much television or playing too many video games?
- Is it possible that physical or medical problems are affecting the student's schoolwork?

- Are there emotional or family problems or changes that could be affecting the student, such as alcohol or drug abuse, family violence, divorce, a recent death, job loss, financial problems, or a new family member?
- How can you, as a parent, assist in finding a remedy or solution for your child?
- Are you able and willing to follow through with the educational recommendations for your child?
- What adjustments at home will be necessary to carry out those recommendations?

School-Related Questions
- What has been tried so far? What's the rationale for each attempt to help?
- What methods seemed to work, and which ones did not?

- What data or measures of progress are available to document the attempts to help this student?
- Under what learning conditions does the student appear to respond best? What are unfavorable conditions?
- What kind of evaluation is needed to determine the specific educational needs of the student? How will that evaluation be obtained?
- What school resources can be used to help remedy the problem? What's the procedure for gaining access to those resources?
- What is the student's unique learning style, and how does that relate to the problem?
- How does the predominant learning style of the teacher compare to that of the student? How does the teacher

adjust to meet the needs of this student?

- What strengths of the student can be used to help him or her accommodate or compensate for his learning needs?
- How does this specific problem area compare to how well the student is doing with the rest of his or her schooling?
- Are other students having similar problems? If so, what are the implications?
- What has the teacher done to attempt to find help for the student?
- If there are problems with reading, what approach to instruction is being used? What approach best meets the needs of this student? Would a combined approach be more appropriate than a one-dimensional strategy?

Remember to be tactful and polite, yet assertive, in raising the school-related questions with your child's teacher. Your goal is to form a cooperative working alliance. Animosity and defensiveness can create walls and negative attitudes that will hinder the process. You also need to be honest and thorough in looking at yourself and your home situation. Take the time to evaluate all possible sources of your child's problems, and remember that there often can be several components to learning difficulties.

Checklist for Identifying Common Symptoms of Learning Disabilities

Begin the diagnosis process with some preliminary observations about the *kind* of difficulties your child is experiencing. Here is a general checklist of the most common

symptoms of learning disabilities. Two or
three of these items probably don't indicate
a learning disability. If five or more are
present, things begin to look suspicious,
and further investigation is warranted. The
items marked with an asterisk (*) often
indicate ADHD. (A more complete treatment of ADHD is found later in this book.)

- Poor letter or word memory*
- Difficulty sounding out words
- Confusion, transposition, or reversal
  of letters, words, or numbers
- Problems in sequencing of letters,
  words, numbers, or ideas
- Difficulty with organizational skills
- Poor auditory memory
- Difficulty with long- and short-term
  memory
- Inability to discriminate between
  letters, numbers, or sounds
- Poor handwriting and copying

- Difficulty with attention in concentration*
- Restlessness, distractibility*
- Impulsivity*
- Doesn't listen well
- Forgets often, loses things*
- Difficulty reading
- Cannot follow multiple directions*
- Difficulty taking tests
- Erratic performance from day to day
- Poor coordination
- Late gross- or fine-motor development
- Difficulty telling time or distinguishing left from right
- Late speech development, immature speech
- Trouble understanding words or concepts
- Trouble naming familiar people or things

- Tends to say one thing, mean another
- Responds inappropriately in many instances
- Adjusts poorly to change
- Problems making and keeping friends
- Low self-esteem and lack of confidence
- Difficult to discipline

Now let's look at how learning disabilities can affect the student's ability to learn.

How Disabilities Affect the Learning Process

Learning can be seen as a sequence of operations, or steps. If a student has a learning disability, one or more of those steps doesn't function as it should. Dr. Larry Silver uses a scheme to describe the various types of disabilities within the learning process. Following is an adaptation of his descriptions of input, integration, memory, and output disabilities.[3]

Input Disabilities

Information arrives at the brain as impulses from our various senses. This central input process is called *perception*. Children who have trouble with *visual input* are identified as having visual perception disabilities.

Such students may have difficulty recognizing the position and shape of what they see. Letters may be reversed or rotated. The letters *d*, *b*, *p*, *q*, and *g* might be confused. Other students may jump over words, read the same line twice, or skip lines. Yet other students may have poor depth perception or distance judgment. They might bump into things, fall over chairs, or knock over drinks.

Students with problems in the area of *auditory input* are said to have auditory perception disabilities. These children may have difficulty understanding because they don't distinguish subtle differences in sounds. They confuse words and phrases that sound alike. Some children find it hard to pick out an auditory figure from its background. Others process sounds slowly and cannot keep up with the flow of conversation.

A student can also have *kinesthetic* or *tactile* disabilities. This category of *sensory input* involves nerve endings in the skin (*tactile input*), in the muscles (*proprioception input*), and in the inner ear (*vestibular input*). If a child has problems with any or all of these sensory inputs, it's called sensory integrative disorder.

Depending on which sensory systems are involved, the child may have problems with tactile sensitivity, body-movement coordination, and adaptation to the position of the body in space. There can also be problems with the child's ability to easily direct his or her body to perform activities in a smooth, coordinated manner and in the right sequence.[4]

Integration Disabilities

Once information reaches the brain, it has to be understood, or integrated. This requires *sequencing, abstraction,* and *organization* activities.

Sequencing deals with the ability to put things in their proper order. A student with a sequencing disability might reverse the order of letters in words, seeing *dog* and reading *god.* Such children are often unable to use single units of a memorized sequence correctly. If asked what day comes after Wednesday, they have to start counting from Sunday to get the answer.

Abstraction refers to the ability to infer meaning from the symbols that arrive in the brain. Students with a problem in this area will read a story and not be able to generalize from it. They may confuse different meanings of the same word used in different ways. They will appear to be literal and concrete in their thinking and will have trouble generalizing concepts from one setting to another. They may have a hard time understanding jokes and are confused by puns or idioms.

Information, once recorded through perception, sequenced, and given meaning or understood, must be organized. That means it's integrated into a constant flow of information and must be related to previously learned material.

Children with an *organization* disability will have difficulty pulling together multiple parts of information into a full or complete concept. They may learn a series of facts without being able to answer general questions that require the use of those facts. Their lives inside and outside the classroom also reflect this disorganization. Their rooms, lockers, and notebooks are chronically a mess, and they have difficulty organizing time and planning ahead.

Memory Disabilities

Once information is perceived by the brain and integrated, it's stored so it can be retrieved later. This storage and retrieval process is called *memory*. Short-term memory retains information briefly while we concentrate on it, like remembering a phone number long enough to dial it. Long-term memory is the process by which we store information we have often repeated, such as one's social security number.

Most memory disabilities appear to affect short-term memory. An example would be children who seem to know their spelling words the night before but can't get most of them correct on a test the next day. On the other hand, these children may surprise you with their ability to recall events or places from long ago.

Output Disabilities

Output refers to the ways in which information comes out of the brain. This occurs by means of spoken language or through such muscle activity as writing, drawing, gesturing, or motor output. Problems communicating can be a result of either a language or motor disability.

The two forms of language used in communication are *spontaneous* language and *demand* language. Spontaneous language is used to initiate speech. The person is able to pick the subject, organize his or her thoughts, and find the correct words. In demand language, speech is required in response to circumstances provided by someone else. In a split second, the person must simultaneously organize, find words, and answer appropriately. A child with a language disability usually doesn't have problems with spontaneous language but will respond hesitantly in demand situations. He or she will pause, ask for the question to be repeated, give a confused answer, or fail to find the right words.

Motor disabilities also fall into two categories. If a child has difficulty coordinating the use of groups of large muscles, such as those in the arms, legs, and trunk, it's called a *gross motor* disability. Difficulty in performing tasks that require coordinating groups of small muscles, such as those in the hand, is called a *fine motor* disability. Gross motor disabilities may cause the child to be clumsy or have trouble with generalized physical activities such as running, climbing, riding a bike, buttoning shirts, or tying shoelaces.

The most common form of fine motor disability shows up in poor handwriting. Children with this problem can give an excellent verbal description of a proposed essay or report, but they produce confused and error-filled written work.

The learning process is complex, and no one understands completely the intricate workings of the brain. But Dr. Silver's model provides a general understanding of how your child learns and where possible problems may exist. The goal is to arrive at a profile that best describes your son or daughter.

Screening for Learning Problems

The underlying causes of learning problems reveal themselves through recognizable symptoms. The following lists should help you identify those symptoms exhibited by your child.

Screening for ADHD

The following checklist is taken from the *Diagnostic and Statistical Manual of Mental Disorders*. To qualify as having a problem (for example, inattention), your child must have a minimum number of specific symptoms that have persisted for at least six months. These symptoms also need to occur to a degree that is maladaptive and inconsistent with the child's developmental level.[5]

Symptoms of Inattention:
- Often fails to give close attention to details or makes careless mistakes in schoolwork, chores, or other activities
- Often has difficulty sustaining attention in tasks or play activities
- Often does not seem to listen when spoken to directly
- Often does not follow through on instructions and fails to finish schoolwork, chores, or duties in the workplace (not due to resistant, oppositional behavior or failure to understand instructions)
- Often has difficulty organizing tasks and activities

- Often avoids, dislikes, or is reluctant to engage in tasks that require sustained mental effort
- Often loses things necessary for tasks or activities
- Is often easily distracted by extraneous stimuli
- Is often forgetful in daily activities

Symptoms of Hyperactivity-Impulsivity:
- Hyperactivity
- Often fidgets with hands or feet or squirms in seat
- Often leaves seat in classroom or in other situations in which remaining seated is expected
- Often runs about or climbs excessively in situations in which it is inappropriate (in adolescents or adults, may be limited to subjective feelings of restlessness)

- Often has difficulty playing or engaging in leisure activities quietly
- Is often "on the go" or acts as if "driven by a motor"
- Often talks excessively
- Impulsivity
- Often blurts out answers before questions have been completed
- Often has difficulty awaiting his or her turn
- Often interrupts or intrudes on others' conversations or games

The following must be true for a possible diagnosis of ADHD: (1) You must find six or more of the symptoms within a category that have persisted for six months or longer; (2) these symptoms must be evident before age seven; (3) there must be some impairment evident in two or more settings, such as school and at home; (4) there must be clear evidence of clinically significant impairment in social, academic, or occupational functioning; and (5) the symptoms must not be a result of other conditions like mental illness, moodiness, or anxiety disorder.

If your child has five or six behaviors in either the inattentive or impulsive-hyperactive categories, you need to pursue a professional opinion.

Screening for Stress

Because each person experiences stress in unique ways, no one list can mention everything your child might display, but the list below is a good start. Many emotional problems can be reflected by these same symptoms. No single symptom is, in itself, an indicator of stress or underlying emotional disturbance. Look instead for clusters of these symptoms that tend to endure for extended periods.

Emotional Signs:
- Appears worked up and excited
- Is worried and anxious
- Has crying spells
- Grinds teeth or clenches jaw
- Feels at loose ends
- Is forgetful and confused
- Has memory loss or lapses
- Has difficulty concentrating; is inattentive and distractible
- Sleeps too much or can't sleep; has nightmares, fitful sleep
- Overeats or doesn't eat
- Snacks excessively
- Is depressed and apathetic
- Does not respond to nurturing efforts or comments
- Is persistently fatigued
- Lowered level of achievement or performance
- Is often grouchy and irritable

- Complains of being dizzy and disoriented
- Makes excessive demands
- Bed wetting or daytime wetting or soiling
- Seems nervous
- Paces about, can't sit still
- Has excessive or irrational fears
- Panicky or anxious
- Clingy or overdependent on caregiver
- Obsessive, repetitive, or ritualistic behavior
- Finger tapping, foot tapping, pencil tapping, or leg tremors
- Continual frowning or scowling
- Anger outbursts, temper tantrums, aggressive acting out

Internal Signs:
- Upset stomach, nausea, "churning" sensation

- Heartburn, acid indigestion
- Intestinal upset, cramps
- Reports fast or irregular heartbeat
- Clammy, cold, or clenched hands
- Lightheaded or faint
- Hot and/or cold spells
- Blood pressure increases
- Loss of breath or uneven breathing pattern
- Feels "tight" all over
- Tingling sensations on skin
- Cold sores in mouth or on lips
- Complains of feeling sick, but with no observable symptoms

Bodily Signs:
- Headaches
- Backaches and other muscular aches
- Low-grade infections
- Generalized body pain
- Hives

- Rash or acne
- Increase of asthma or allergies
- Constipation or diarrhea
- Coughing, habitual clearing of throat, or vocalizations
- Dry mouth or throat
- Tight and stiff muscles
- Certain muscles begin to twitch; facial tics
- Stuttering or stammering
- Inability to stand still or stay in one place
- Hands shake
- Onset of poor vision
- Increased perspiring

If your child demonstrates more than three or four of these signs with a frequency of once a week or so, there's a strong possibility that he or she is experiencing high stress levels. Emotional problems could be part of the total picture as well.

Screening for Depression

A combination of certain behavioral changes and disturbances in mood can suggest a depressive disorder. The symptoms should last for at least two weeks and should represent a departure from the way your child usually acts. If five or more of the following symptoms seem to describe how your child is behaving, depression is possible.

Symptoms of Depression

- Depressed or irritable mood most of the time; reports feeling sad or empty; appears angry, grouchy, or easily offended
- Loss of interest or pleasure in most things he or she used to enjoy doing

- Increase or decrease in appetite or weight loss or gain
- Sleep disturbance such as insomnia (too little sleep) or hypersomnia (too much sleep), difficulty getting to sleep, or frequent nightmares
- Activity level is either up or down
- Fatigue or loss of energy
- Guilt or feelings of worthlessness, low self-esteem, hopelessness, and pessimism
- Diminished ability to think or concentrate; may include indecisiveness
- Recurrent thoughts of death and/or suicide[6]
- Frequent complaints of vague, nonspecific physical symptoms such as headaches, muscle aches, stomachaches, or tiredness
- Frequent absences from school or poor performance when there

- Refusal to go to school
- Clinging to parent
- Worry that parent or other family member may die
- Talking about running away from home, or attempting to do so
- Outbursts of shouting, complaining, unexplained irritability, or crying
- Boredom
- Lack of interest in playing with friends
- Alcohol or substance abuse
- Abnormal fear of death
- Extreme sensitivity to rejection or failure
- Increased irritability, anger, or hostility
- Reckless behavior
- Difficulty with relationships[7]

Many situations can lead to depression in a child, including the separation or divorce of parents, the death of a loved one, a move or a change in schools, academic failure, illness or injury, and many others. The common element in these experiences is a sense of loss. From these feelings, depression can emerge.

Sometimes the symptoms of depression are present, but no predisposing events are evident. However, a child may internalize traumatic events without telling others. Good examples are critical comments made by a teacher or other child, and secret abuse. If you can't relate your child's symptoms of depression to significant events, the help of a mental health professional and/or a medical practitioner may be crucial.

Screening for Abuse

Research suggests that neglected and abused children perform worse on standardized tests, receive lower grades, are more likely to repeat a grade, and have more discipline referrals than other children. Poor language skills and achievement levels can result from chronic or severe abuse.

To help you make an initial determination of whether your child or others you know have suffered abuse, checklists of symptoms often seen in abused children are presented below.[8]

These are not comprehensive lists, but these are some common symptoms of abuse. Keep in mind that although physical and/or sexual abuse can contribute to learning problems, it accounts for a small percentage of all such problems. In addition, just because a child may seem to exhibit a few symptoms does not necessarily indicate abuse. For more information and more comprehensive checklists, go to www.drgrantmartin.com/links.html.

Symptoms of Sexual Abuse:

A trauma such as sexual abuse is certain to result in some type of symptoms. Usually, there are no clear physical signs, so the child himself or herself is the best (and sometimes *only*) source of warning signals. These behavioral signs will vary according to the age of the child.

- Indirect hints or open statements about abuse
- Difficulty in peer relationships and violence against younger children
- Withdrawn, less verbal, depressed or apathetic
- Abrupt and drastic personality changes
- Self-mutilation
- Preoccupation with death, guilt, heaven, or hell
- Anger, acting out, disobedience

- Refusal to be left with potential offender or caretaker
- Retreat to fantasy world or dissociative reactions—loss of memory, imaginary playmates, child uses more than one name
- Sudden increase in modesty
- Becoming uncomfortable around or hostile toward persons they used to trust
- Runaway behavior or stated desire to live elsewhere
- Extreme fear or repulsion when touched by an adult of either sex
- Onset of poor personal hygiene, attempts to make self appear unattractive
- Sophisticated sexual knowledge or provocative sexual behavior
- Regression to earlier, infant behavior—bed wetting, thumb sucking

- Sleep disturbances, nightmares, or change in sleep habits
- Continual, unexplained fear, anxiety, or panic
- Onset of eating disorders—anorexia, bulimia, compulsive eating
- Inability to concentrate in school, hyperactive
- Sudden drop in school performance

Symptoms of Domestic Violence:
- The children act opposite to previous patterns.
- They act out rather than withdraw.
- They're aggressive rather than passive.
- They refuse to go to school.
- They overachieve rather than under-achieve.
- Bed wetting and nightmares are common.

- They take on a caretaking role, more concerned for others than self, become parent substitutes.
- They develop rigid defenses: aloof, sarcastic, defensive, polarized thinking.
- They use excessive attention-seeking behavior, often using extreme behaviors.
- They're out of control, not able to set own limits or follow directions, may mimic ADHD.[9]

Screening for Underachievement

The symptoms of underachievement are reasonably easy to spot. The following checklist identifies the most common indicators.

- Poor grades compared to known ability or potential

- Inadequate motivation
- Apathy
- Performance below expectations or ability
- Low evaluations by teachers or coaches
- Preoccupation with activities unrelated to academics or other areas of concern
- Irritation, anger, or defiance when confronted with lack of effort
- Denial of existence of homework when asked
- Low self-esteem, sense of inferiority
- Self-deprecating attitude
- Lack of initiative to change or try new solutions
- Refusal to pursue more challenging courses, skills, or competition
- Inability to persevere
- Emotional immaturity

- Lack of personal, academic, physical, or spiritual goals

Often there are combinations of reasons why the student isn't motivated to work up to his or her capacity. Once a parent has observed three or four of the above symptoms, he or she should move to the next level of evaluation.

Obtaining a Professional Diagnosis

It can often be difficult to pinpoint exactly what a child's learning problem is without a professional opinion. As you've seen, the same symptoms may be caused by any of a number of underlying problems, or by a combination of problems. If any of the previous checklists or descriptions seems to apply to your child, the next step may be to pursue a professional diagnosis.

Medical Exam

One of the first steps in the evaluation process is to rule out any medical problems that could be affecting your student's learning. Your child should have a complete physical exam, as well as thorough vision and hearing evaluations.

The usual physical exams required for school may not show anything if the child is otherwise healthy. Be sure your physician knows you are concerned about your child's learning process. Explain the nature of the school problems and how the child behaves outside the doctor's office.

Psychological Evaluation

Emotional contributions to learning problems can be evaluated by a mental health professional such as a child psychiatrist or psychologist, as well as by social workers and child therapists. Emotions, brain function, learning style, and environment interact in wonderfully complex ways. Be prepared for difficulties in identifying precisely all the causes of your child's learning problems.

Educational Evaluation

If your child attends a public school, ask the classroom teacher how to initiate a referral to have your child evaluated. Often the teacher will bring up the concern in the first place, so he or she will undoubtedly have a plan for starting the process.

In most schools, a "focus of concern" process is used to evaluate a student and determine eligibility for services. A focus of concern can be initiated by school personnel or parents. Each district is supposed to have the process spelled out so parents know exactly what will be done and on what schedule.

Even if your child attends a private school or home school, as a taxpayer you still have access to the services of the public school for the assessment. The procedure is the same. You fill out the focus-of-concern request at the local school your child would ordinarily attend. Your child's private-school or home-school teacher will then need to supply some basic performance information.

You may want to seek an evaluation with a private clinician or organization. If you do, be sure to find someone who has the necessary credentials and experience. You can ask the school for a list of professionals who specialize in this area, or contact one of the organizations listed at the end of this book.

Be sure to inquire about costs. A basic evaluation may cost several hundred dollars, while a complicated case may cost several thousand. Sometimes you can get an excellent evaluation at a lower cost from a university because your case is used for training purposes. Also, ask your insurance carrier if it covers the cost of testing. If you have had an evaluation done by the school but aren't satisfied, it might be possible for the school to pay for a second opinion—though not if the school considers its evaluation appropriate.

Treatment
for Learning
Problems

B y now you've probably identified some of your child's learning problems. I encourage you to seek the help needed for your child and to network with professionals and other parents with expertise and experience. As you do, you'll hear about various treatment options. The following summaries outline key guidelines to pursuing help for a variety of challenges.

Treatment for Learning Disabilities

Treatment for learning disabilities starts with the professional evaluation and individualized education program (IEP) that addresses your child's specific learning difficulties. Keep in mind that there are no perfect programs for all learning disabled (LD) students. A program is appropriate only to the extent to which the instruction and services address the needs of your particular child.

However, the effort to help your child doesn't end when the plan is in place. There is much that parents can do to support their LD child. It's helpful to remember that these students always have some positive features. Remember your child's laudable and lovable characteristics when you feel discouraged about his or her challenges. Here are some guidelines for parents seeking to help children with learning disabilities:

- Treat your child as a capable human being.
- Focus on what your child *can* do, not on what he or she *can't* do.
- Respect and challenge your child's natural intelligence.
- Let your child know you enjoy spending time with him or her.

- Discuss with your child some of your own struggles as a student.
- Teach and model that mistakes don't equal failure.
- It's important to acknowledge the *effort* toward a goal as well as its achievement.
- Communicate the concept that this is a family effort.
- Love your child unconditionally.
- Accept your child as he or she is. Don't compare him or her with brothers and sisters or classmates.
- Be realistic in your expectations for what your child can do now, but don't ever put a ceiling on what your child can eventually do or be.
- Challenge your child to take responsibility for his or her actions.
- Encourage problem solving at every opportunity.

- Be aware that struggling with your child over reading, writing, math, and homework can create an adversarial relationship.
- Make sure books are at your child's reading level.
- Keep to a regular routine.
- Take care of yourself to prevent burnout.
- Maintain your sense of humor.

Space does not allow a detailed presentation of various educational methodologies for helping LD students. But if you're interested in more details, be sure to consult some of the books and Web sites listed in the resource section.

A detailed description of various approaches to both accommodation and remediation techniques can be found in *Help! for Teachers: Strategies for Reaching All Students*. Accommodation is helping a student use certain of his strengths to overcome the weaker areas of learning. Remediation is helping bring weak areas of learning up to at least average levels by focused and systematic instruction.

Treatment for Attention-Deficit/ Hyperactivity Disorder

There's no cure or quick fix for attention disorders. Despite claims to the contrary, special diets, electronic gadgets, and singular environmental alterations have not been proved to be helpful for significant numbers of ADHD children. The good news, however, is that there are numerous strategies and procedures that can improve your child's behavior, self-esteem, and overall quality of life. ADHD children need clear *structure*, definite *descriptions* of what they're being asked to do, specific *consequences* for their behavior, and consistent *enforcement* of those principles. They need an organized environment where the demands of a specific situation are identified ahead of time, and lots of rewards and praise are given for successful and appropriate behavior.[10]

The next category of intervention is to help your child utilize more of what he or she knows about self-control and positive social interactions. ADHD children must learn to take control of their reactions. We can help them learn to control movement, set the idle lower, and put a limit on impulses. Various games and activities such as Statue, Beat the Clock, endurance, calmness, and impulse-control training, along with learning how to ignore distractions, can be used.[11]

One of the most difficult decisions the parents of an ADHD child will face is whether to use medication. More research has been conducted on the effects of stimulant medications on the functioning of children with ADHD than on any other treatment for any childhood problem. This extensive research helps us be fairly definitive about the benefits and liabilities of medication.

In general, we can say medication intervention is a significant help to ADHD children. However, a great deal of misinformation has been perpetuated by the popular press and some special-interest groups. Yes, it's true that on occasion medications are improperly prescribed and monitored. That's why it's important to have a professional evaluation to determine whether your child actually has ADHD. If medication is considered, it must follow strict controls, appropriate dosages, and careful monitoring.

ADHD can be viewed as a result of a

malfunction of the attention system. That system allows the brain to distinguish situations where focused, deliberate behavior is appropriate from situations where quick, impulsive actions are needed. Medication works to enhance the functioning of the attention system so that children can choose when to be sensitive to outside distractions and when to focus their attention. The attention center is stimulated by these medications, with the result that the children have better control.[12] Medication won't make your child behave perfectly, nor will it make him or her smarter. But it can reduce many of your child's attention difficulties so he or she can tackle problems more successfully.

The decision to proceed with medication intervention must be based on a comparison of the risks, benefits, and alternative treatments available. You and your physician will need to decide based on the advantages of decreased distractibility versus side effects. If the dosage is carefully monitored and adjusted, medication has been found to enhance academic performance. But remember that medication is never the sole treatment for ADHD. Medical, behavioral, psychological, and educational interventions are not adequate by themselves. We must be conscious of treating the *whole* person.

Helping Your Child Deal with Stress

Burnout occurs when the demands of a situation overwhelm a child's ability to deal with the event or accumulation of events. When the stressors are too much, some of the signs listed on page 40-45 will appear. That begins the process of coping with stress.

1. Be aware of what's happening within your child and the environment.
2. Develop a positive perspective about stressors.
3. Practice healthy living habits (adequate sleep, healthful meals, physical fitness opportunities).
4. Teach your children how to relax using the following steps. With practice, this simple procedure can be helpful in lowering stress:
   a. Become aware that something is bothering you.
   b. Make a deliberate effort to relax your facial muscles. Relax your forehead, eyes, nose, and mouth (as well as your neck). Try smiling to help your face relax.
   c. Take a long, deep breath, then exhale slowly, letting your jaw go limp.
5. Reduce or eliminate possible stressors.

Dr. Archibald Hart gives five important principles regarding stress inoculation in his book *Stress and Your Child*. They're summarized here:

- Gradually expose children to problems.
- Resist the urge to rescue. Gradually back off and let them take more responsibility for creating solutions to their own problems.
- Teach healthy self-talk by helping them rephrase their faulty thinking with rational and honest thoughts.
- Teach children to allow adequate time for recovery from periods of too much stress.
- Teach children to ask themselves, when confronted with a problem, "Is this really that big a deal?" This can help them keep out unneeded concerns for things that aren't that critical.[13]

The presence of protective factors in family, school, and community environments appears to alter or reverse negative outcomes of stress and to foster the development of resiliency. Those protective factors are:

- A caring and supportive relationship with at least one person
- Consistently clear, high expectations communicated to the child
- Ample opportunities to participate in and contribute meaningfully to one's social environment.[14]

How to Help a Depressed Child

If you think one of your children is depressed, again the first step is a complete physical exam. If the doctor rules out medical sources of depression such as diabetes, thyroid problems, toxins, or a brain tumor, the next step is to explore the psychological sources for the depression by consulting with a mental health professional. Take along a copy of the checklist of the symptoms of depression, and have in mind possible sources of your child's feelings, so you can discuss them with the therapist.

A variety of methods may be used in the diagnostic process. It will be important to rule out coexisting conditions such as learning disabilities, attention deficits, or other emotional features such as mood disorders. After the counselor makes a diagnosis, treatment may involve individual therapy for the child, sessions with the entire family, or a combination. It all depends on the needs of the child.

How to Help a Child of Divorce

There's no way to get through divorce without some pain and suffering. Therefore, the goal is to minimize the damage and do everything possible to support the children. How can parents help?

- Try to reconcile the marriage, if possible.
- Provide age-appropriate reasons for the divorce, along with forecasting the process of events. Provide assurance that your children's basic needs will be met.
- Don't make promises you can't keep.
- It's crucial to assure kids that the divorce or separation is not their fault.
- Help your children verbalize their feelings. They need to talk about their distress, anger, and anxiety. A chance to grieve is critical.
- Give appropriate reassurances.
- A support system is vital. Don't be afraid to ask for assistance from

extended family, church family, and others.

- Maintain consistency in routine.
- It may seem contradictory, but the more the parents can agree about issues in the parenting plan, the better children will adjust to the realities of divorce.

Make sure your children's teachers know about the situation. Caring teachers are in a position to reassure students and help them learn to cope. They can work to make their classrooms as stable and predictable as possible and help children feel a sense of control.

How to Help an Abused Child

Here are some general ideas of how intervention will progress in cases where children have been victimized.

- The first priority is to stop the abuse. That may mean using legal procedures to remove the perpetrator, followed by a host of legal, social, economic, and emotional actions.
- The victim and the family will need therapy and education.
- Instruction in social skills is often needed.
- Attention to negative thought patterns that accompany depression and feelings of helplessness is usually required.
- The second major priority of intervention is to *break the cycle* of violence and abuse. There are no simple ways to do this, but in the case of domestic voilence, limiting violent TV programming, toys, and games will help. Above all, we need to

model and teach nonviolent ways to deal with anger and show children alternative ways to handle their aggressiveness.

- Within domestic-violence situations, all the issues relating to spouse abuse need attention.
- Prevention of further abuse is the final priority.

The majority of abused children will need some type of medical and/or psychological help. Counseling is important for victims of abuse and their families. However, seeking the healing touch of God is most crucial of all. To pursue this topic in more detail, please refer to the resource list on pages 93-99. If you suspect that your child is being abused or you are living with domestic voilence, please call 1-800-AFAMILY (1-800-232-6459) between

9:00 A.M. and 4:30 P.M. Mountain Time for a referral to a counselor in your area or to speak to one of our counselors.

How to Help an Underachieving Child

If your child is not achieving, first look at your expectations. No student should be expected to produce at remarkable levels all the time. Below are six principles about capable children to keep in mind.

1. Remember that the real basics go beyond reading, writing, and arithmetic.
2. They can be good at something they don't enjoy doing.
3. They can be good at some things that are unpopular with their friends.
4. Don't allow them to become preoccupied with performance, work, or success, and don't be afraid to let them try

something in which they might not succeed.

5. Encourage them to ask questions that should have answers but don't.

6. Emphasize that they always have career options and can pursue the goals they want most.[15]

Next, understand your child's learning abilities. Is there any chance a limitation or disability may be present? Review the questions and procedures provided earlier in this book to see if a more comprehensive evaluation is needed.

Evaluate the classroom situation in view of your child's learning style, strengths, and weaknesses. A young, curious student may easily become "turned off" if the educational environment is not stimulating or if class placement and teaching approaches are inappropriate. Lack of motivation can also occur if the child has ineffective teachers, or if assignments are consistently too difficult or too easy. Providing an early and appropriate educational environment can stimulate a love for learning.

The third part of your action plan is to look for ways to encourage and motivate your underachieving student. The key to unlocking your children's potential is to cultivate the dormant seed of interest. Provide them with a wide variety of opportunities for success, a sense of accomplishment, and a belief in themselves. Encourage your children to volunteer to help others as an avenue for developing tolerance, empathy, understanding, and acceptance of their limitations.

Many capable children need reasonable rules and guidelines, strong encouragement, consistently positive feedback, and help to accept some limitations—

their own, as well as those of others. They should be strongly encouraged to pursue their interests, particularly since those interests may lead to career decisions and lifelong passions. Providing real-world experiences in an area of potential career interest may also provide motivation toward academic achievement.

When problem solving is appropriate, encourage students to come up with their own answers and criteria for choosing the best solution. Show genuine enthusiasm for your child's observations, interests, activities, and goals.

Whether a capable youngster uses exceptional ability in constructive ways depends, in part, on self-acceptance and self-concept. According to one expert, "an intellectually gifted child will not be happy and complete until s/he is using intellectual ability at a level approaching full capacity. . . .

It is important that parents and teachers see intellectual development as a requirement for these children, and not merely as an interest or a phase they will outgrow."[16]

Should Your Child Be Retained?

Retention has often been used for students who are lagging behind academically or who appear more immature than their peers. The question is whether this attempt to help students actually works. The answer is, generally speaking, *no*. We need to intervene with tutoring, incentive or motivational plans, and remedial instruction meant to address the reasons the students are having difficulty.[17]

Though retention generally doesn't work, there are exceptions. Under what conditions might retention with other accommodations and interventions be appropriate for *your* child? Here are some considerations:

- Have your child tested. If he or she is cognitively capable of completing the work, retention is not the answer.
- If your child is physically small and has a birthday near the school district's cutoff date for first grade, retention may be appropriate, but other conditions must also apply. Size alone is not a sufficient reason for retention.
- Emotional maturity isn't likely to be helped by retention alone.
- Develop a complete plan for remedial services.
- How well will your child fit with the proposed teacher? The teaching style and expectations of next year's

teacher will make a significant impact on your child.

- How would retention affect the family?
- Is there a possibility the school is motivated to retain the child based on economic considerations?
- If your child faces the possibility of being retained, there must be a total appraisal of the classroom learning environment, with appropriate suggestions also being made to the teacher and specific intervention approaches being instituted.[18]

If retention seems to have merit, the major consideration must be the development and implementation of a teaching and treatment plan that will concentrate on the deficit areas of the child.

Conclusion

Parents always need to keep the big picture in view when evaluating an educational program. Goals for education should touch on the following areas: intellectual, social, emotional, physical, and spiritual. Parents shouldn't expect the school to accomplish all their educational goals, of course. But you need to have a clear idea of what you want your children to get out of school in order to evaluate completely how they're progressing.

This book is a quick overview and reference to help you identify your child's learning problems and acquaint you with the various treatment options that are available. It is not a comprehensive guide. Therefore, there's a list of helpful resources at the end of this book to take you to the next step. Assistance *is* available. Whatever the nature of your child's learning problem, there's a lot that trained, experienced, caring professionals can do for him or her. Follow the procedures described in this book to get that help.

And finally, *never give up*—on your child, on his or her potential, or on your duty to be your child's biggest fan and advocate. God *will* sustain you in this vital part of your job as a parent.

Notes

1. Cynthia Ulrich Tobias, *The Way They Learn: How to Discover and Teach to Your Child's Strengths* (Colorado Springs, Colo.: Focus on the Family, 1994), 14-19.
2. Grant L. Martin, *Counseling in Cases of Family Violence and Abuse*, vol. 6 (Dallas: Word, 1987), 125-54.
3. Larry B. Silver, "A Look at Learning Disabilities in Children and Youth," *Learning Disability Association of Montgomery County Newsletter* 22, 2 (Nov. 1991), 3-5. Used with permission of Learning Disability Association of Montgomery County, Inc., P.O. Box 623, Rockville, MD 20848-0623; phone: (301) 933-1076. Larry B. Silver, "What are Learning Disabilities?" LDOnline, (November, 2001) http://www.ldonline.org/ld_indepth/general_info/what_are_ld_silver.html.
4. Larry B. Silver, *The Misunderstood Child: Guide for Parents of Learning Disabled Children*, 2d ed. (Blue Ridge Summit, Pa.: TAB Books, 1992), 30.

5. American Psychiatric Association, *Diagnostic and Statistical Manual of Mental Disorders*, 4th ed. (Washington, D.C.: American Psychiatric Association, 1994), 83-84. Used by permission.

6. Ibid., 327. Used by permission.

7. National Institute of Mental Health, "Depression in Children and Adolescents." Bethesda, Md.: National Institute of Mental Health, 2000. http://www.nimh.nih.gov/publicat/depchildresfact.cfm.

8. Grant L. Martin, *Critical Problems in Children and Youth: Counseling Techniques for Problems Resulting from Attention Deficit Disorder, Sexual Abuse, Custody Battles, and Related Issues* (Dallas: Word, 1992), 100-104.

9. Audrey Mitchell, *Domestic/Dating Violence: An Information and Resource Handbook* (Seattle: Metropolitan King County Council, 1994), 13. Used by permission.

10. Grant L. Martin, *The Hyperactive Child: What You Need to Know About Attention-Deficit Hyperactivity Disorder* (Wheaton, Ill.: Victor Books, 1992, 1998); Larry B. Silver, *Dr. Larry Silver's Advice to Parents on Attention-Deficit Hyperactivity Disorder* (Washington, D.C.: American Psychiatric Press, 1993); Sam Goldstein and Michael Goldstein, *Hyperactivity:*

Why Won't My Child Pay Attention? (New York: John Wiley and Sons, 1992); Stephen W. Garber, Marianne D. Garber, and Robyn F. Spizman, *If Your Child Is Hyperactive, Inattentive, Impulsive, Distractible . . . Helping the ADD Hyperactive Child* (New York: Villard Books, 1990).

11. Garber, Garber, and Spizman, *If Your Child Is Hyperactive*, 89-151.

12. Sam Goldstein and Michael Goldstein, *Managing Attention Disorders in Children* (New York: John Wiley and Sons, 1990), 256-58.

13. Archibald D. Hart, *Stress and Your Child* (Dallas: Word, 1992), 121-26. Used by permission. All rights reserved.

14. B. Benard, *Fostering Resiliency in Kids: Protective Factors in the Family, School, and Community* (Portland, Ore.: Western Center for Drug-Free Schools and Communities, ERIC document 335 781, 1991).

15. J. R. Delisle, *Guiding the Social and Emotional Development of Gifted Youth: A Practical Guide for Educators and Counselors* (New York: Longman, 1992), 137-45. Adapted with permission.

16. J. W. Halsted, *Guiding Gifted Readers—From Preschool to High School* (Columbus, Ohio: Ohio Psychology Publishing, 1988), 24.

17. S. E. Peterson, J. S. DeGracie, and C. R. Ayabe, "A Longitudinal Study of the Effects of Retention/Promotion on Academic Achievement," *American Educational Research Journal* 24 (1987): 107-18. National Association of School Psychologists, "Position Statement on Student Grade Retention and Social Promotion, 2003. http://www.nasponline.org /information/pospaper_graderetent.html.
18. Gilbert R. Gredler, *School Readiness: Assessment and Educational Issues* (Brandon, Vt.: Clinical Psychology Publishing Co., 1992), 260.

Resources

ORGANIZATIONS

American Speech-Language-Hearing Association
  (ASHA)
1801 Rockville Pike
Rockville, MD 20852
(800) 638-8255; (301) 897-5700; www.asha.org

Applied Learning Styles
P.O. Box 1450
Sumner, WA 98390
(253) 891-8581 (Fax); www.applest.com

Attention Deficit Disorder Association (ADDA)
P.O. Box 543
Pottstown, PA 19464
(484) 945-2101; www.add.org

Autism Society of America (formerly NSAC)
7910 Woodmont Avenue, Suite 300
Bethesda, MD 20814-3067
(800) 3-AUTISM; (301) 657-0881;
  www.autism-society.org

Children and Adults with Attention-Deficit/
   Hyperactivity Disorder (CHADD)
8181 Professional Place, Suite 150
Landover, MD 20785
(301) 306-7070; (800) 233-4050;
   www.chadd.org

Christian Legal Society
8001 Braddock Road, Suite 300
Springfield, VA 22151
(703) 642-1070; www.clsnet.org

Eagle Forum Education & Legal Defense Fund
7800 Bonhomme
St. Louis, MO 63105
(314) 721-1213; www.eagleforum.org

Learning Disabilities Association of America
   (LDA)
4156 Library Road
Pittsburg, PA 15234
(412) 341-1515; www.ldaamerica.org

National Association for Gifted Children
1707 L Street N.W., Suite 550
Washington, DC 20036
(202) 785-4268; www.nagc.org

National Center for Learning Disabilities (NCLD)
381 Park Avenue S, Suite 1401
New York, NY 10016-8806
(212) 545-7510; www.ncld.org

National Dissemination Center for Children
   with Disabilities (NICHCY)
P.O. Box 1492
Washington, DC 20013
(800) 695-0285; (202) 884-8441;
   www.nichcy.org

National Institute for Learning Disabilities
   (NILD)
107 Seekel Street
Norfolk, VA 23505
(877) 661-6453; (757) 423-8646; www.nild.net

National Right to Read Foundation
P.O. Box 490
The Plains, VA 20198
(540) 349-1614; www.nrrf.org

The Gifted Child Society
190 Rock Road
Glen Rock, NJ 07452-1736
(210) 444-6530; www.gifted.org

The International Dyslexia Association
Chester Building, Suite 382
8600 La Salle Road
Baltimore, MD 21286-2044
(410) 296-0232, Ext. 126; www.interdys.org

U.S. National Library of Medicine (MedLine Plus)
8699 Rockville Pike
Bethesda, MD 20894
www.nlm.nih.gov/medlineplus/childabuse.html

ONLINE RESOURCES

www.ldonline.com—A major Web site on learning disabilities and ADHD. Information is provided for educators, parents, and kids.

www.schwablearning.org—A parents' guide to helping children with learning disabilities.

www.ncld.org/content/view/827/527/—The resources offered in National Center for Learning Disabilities New Parent Center are for parents of a child with a learning disability (LD), or for parents who suspect their child may have a learning disability. The Parent Center offers a comprehensive guide to the Individuals with Disabilities Education Act (IDEA), short guides, articles, and much more.

BOOKS

Learning Disabilities

Huston, Anne Marshall. *Understanding Dyslexia: A Practical Handbook for Parents and Teachers.* Landham, Md.: Madison Books, 2000.

Ingersoll, Barbara D., and Sam Goldstein. *Attention Deficit Disorder and Learning Disabilities: Reality, Myths, and Controversial Treatments.* New York: Doubleday, 1993.

Learning Disabilities Council. *Understanding Learning Disabilities: A Parent Guide and Workbook.* Richmond, Va.: Learning Disabilities Council, 1991.

Silver, Larry B. *The Misunderstood Child: A Guide for Parents of Learning Disabled Children.* Three Rivers, Mich.: Three Rivers Press, 1998.

Attention-Deficit/Hyperactivity Disorder (ADHD)

Garber, S. W., M. D. Garber, and R. F. Spizman. *Is Your Child Hyperactive? Inattentive? Impulsive? Distractible? Helping the ADD/Hyperactive Child.* New York: Villard Books, 1995.

Goldstein, S., and M. Goldstein. *Hyperactivity: Why Won't My Child Pay Attention?* New York: John Wiley and Sons, 1993.

Ingersoll, Barbara D., and Sam Goldstein. *Attention Deficit Disorder and Learning Disabilities: Reality, Myths, and Controversial Treatments.* New York: Doubleday, 1993.

Martin, Grant L. *The Attention Deficit Child: What You Need to Know about Attention-Deficit/Hyperactivity Disorder—Facts, Myths, and Treatment*. Colorado Springs, Colo.: Cook Communications, 1998.

Swanberg, Dennis, and Diane Passno with medical contributions by Walt Larimore, M.D. *Why A.D.H.D. Doesn't Mean Disaster*. Carol Stream, Ill.: Tyndale House Publishers, 2003.

Emotional Problems Caused by Stress, Divorce, or Sexual Abuse

Allender, Dan. *The Wounded Heart: Hope for Adult Victims of Childhood Sexual Abuse*. Colorado Springs, Colo.: NavPress, 1990.

Barr, Debbie. *Children of Divorce: Helping Kids When Their Parents Are Apart*. Grand Rapids: Zondervan, 1992.

Hart, Dr. Archibald. *Helping Children Survive Divorce*. Nashville: W Publishing Group, 1997.

Heitritter, Lynn and Jeanette Vought. *Helping Victims of Sexual Abuse: A Sensitive, Biblical Guide for Counselors, Victims and Families*. Minneapolis: Bethany House Publishers, 2006.

Swenson, Richard A. *A Minute of Margin: Restoring Balance to Busy Lives*. Colorado Springs, Colo.: NavPress, 2003.

Legal Issues
Cutler, Barbara Coyne. *You, Your Child, and "Special" Education*. Baltimore: Brookes Publishing, 1995.

General Education Issues
Martin, Grant L. *Help! for Teachers: Strategies for Reaching All Students*. Colorado Springs, Colo.: Purposeful Design Publications, 2004.

Sheble, Jan. *School Choices: What's Best for Your Child*. Kansas City, Mo.: Beacon Hill Press, 2003.

Tobias, Cynthia Ulrich. *The Way They Learn*. Carol Stream, Ill.: Tyndale House Publishers, 1998.

FOCUS ON THE FAMILY BROADCASTS
Dobson, Dr. James and panel. "Attention Deficit Disorder," CD144.

Fuller, Cheri. "Motivating Your Child to Learn," CS560.

Martin, Dr. Grant and Grace Mutzabaugh. "Learning Difficulties," CD944.

Schimmels, Dr. Cliff. "Kids and School," CD520.

Tobias, Cynthia. "Learning Styles," CD237.

BOOKLETS FROM FOCUS ON THE FAMILY
Evans, Jamie. "Learning Disabilities," FX018.

Focus on the Family. "Gifted Children," FX004.

Martin, Grant L. "Attention Deficit Disorders," LF223/12440.

Dr. Bill Maier is Focus on the Family's vice president and psychologist in residence. Dr. Maier received his master's and doctoral degrees from the Rosemead School of Psychology at Biola University in La Mirada, California. A child and family psychologist, Dr. Maier hosts the national "Weekend Magazine" radio program and the "Family Minute with Dr. Bill Maier." He also acts as a media spokesperson for Focus on the Family on a variety of family-related issues. He and his wife, Lisa, have been married for more than seven years and have two children.

9 9 9

Dr. Grant L. Martin is a licensed psychologist and marriage and family therapist in Edmonds, Washington with more than 37 years of experience. He is an expert in the special needs of children, including learning problems and related issues. He has authored 14 books including *Help! for Teachers, Critical Problems in Children and Youth,* and *The Attention Deficit Child.* Dr. Martin appears frequently on radio talk shows and TV programs. He and his wife, Jane, have been married for more than 40 years and have two sons and two grandchildren.

FOCUS ON THE FAMILY®

Welcome to the family!

Whether you purchased this book, borrowed it, or received it as a gift, we're glad you're reading it. It's just one of the many helpful, encouraging, and biblically based resources produced by Focus on the Family for people in all stages of life.

Focus began in 1977 with the vision of one man, Dr. James Dobson, a licensed psychologist and author of numerous best-selling books on marriage, parenting, and family. Alarmed by the societal, political, and economic pressures that were threatening the existence of the American family, Dr. Dobson founded Focus on the Family with one employee and a once-a-week radio broadcast aired on 36 stations.

Now an international organization reaching millions of people daily, Focus on the Family is dedicated to preserving values and strengthening and encouraging families through the life-changing message of Jesus Christ.

Focus on the Family Magazines

These faith-building, character-developing publications address the interests, issues, concerns, and challenges faced by every member of your family from preschool through the senior years.

| Focus on the Family Citizen® U.S. news issues | Focus on the Family Clubhouse Jr.® Ages 4 to 8 | Focus on the Family Clubhouse™ Ages 8 to 12 | Breakaway® Teen guys | Brio® Teen girls 12 to 16 | Brio & Beyond® Teen girls 16 to 19 | Plugged In® Reviews movies, music, TV |

FOR MORE INFORMATION

Online:
Log on to www.family.org
In Canada, log on to
www.focusonthefamily.ca

Phone:
Call toll free: (800) A-FAMILY
In Canada, call toll free:
(800) 661-9800

More Great Resources
from Focus on the Family®

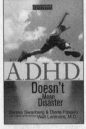